The Clink
VEGETABLES
Cookbook

For prisoners to be successfully rehabilitated and to contribute
to a better society for all, they don't only need to stop offending.
They need shelter and food, training, employment, motivation,
confidence, compassion, self-esteem and moral support.
All of these are provided by The Clink, to ensure prisoners
have the best possible chance of turning their lives around.

Alberto Crisci MBE,
Founder of The Clink

The Clink
VEGETABLES
Cookbook

All recipes by Al Crisci, unless otherwise credited

THE
CLINK
CHARITY

CONTENTS

Christopher Moore
Chief Executive

Changing attitudes, transforming lives and creating second chances

As I write, there are 84,000 adults in prison in England and Wales. Of those released, sadly 49% are reconvicted within a year. The aim of The Clink Charity is to reduce reoffending by training our graduates and placing them into jobs in the hospitality industry. A 2018 report shows that prisoners going through our training are 49.6% less likely to reoffend.

We launched the first Clink Restaurant in 2009 and now have four restaurants, at HMP High Down, HMP Cardiff, HMP Brixton and HMP Styal, as well as a café off prison grounds in Manchester. By dining with us, you are supporting our training and giving the prisoners the experience they require.

During the last 12 months, The Clink has trained up to 200 prisoners a day, issued 106 City & Guilds certificates and served an astounding 100,000 diners.

Prisoners at the Clink work a 40-hour week in conditions that simulate a professional environment. Our trainers help them gain City & Guilds National Vocational Qualifications (NVQs). On their release, support workers help

them find jobs and housing, then mentor them, helping them reintegrate into society. There are more than 280 employers now willing to take on a Clink graduate, and we've won more than 60 awards. Our ambassadors include Prue Leith, Cyrus Todiwala and Giorgio Locatelli.

We also operate Clink Gardens at HMP Send and HMP High Down, where we train prisoners to achieve NVQs in horticulture. Fruit, vegetables and herbs from the gardens are used in the restaurants, along with eggs from our chickens; that is what has inspired this, our fourth book.

Our aim is for more than 1,500 graduates to enter jobs each year by 2020. We are proud that, with our partner HM Prison and Probation Service, we achieve extraordinary outcomes while reducing reoffending, in a value-for-money way, with compassion and integrity, in an environment that sometimes seems bleak, with many daily challenges.

The Clink shows what can be achieved when society engages collectively to help those who want and deserve a second chance.

Finlay Scott
Chairman and
Founder Trustee

When we published this book, The Clink had four excellent restaurants, two garden projects, a café and an outside event catering enterprise. We have exciting plans to open more restaurants and to expand into bakery and other craft-based industries. The focus of our Charity is to train prisoners in cooking, food preparation and service, then to help them into work upon leaving prison. This has, over the last eight years, produced remarkable outcomes with the 1,300 trainees who have gone through our programme, leading to a reduction in reoffending, less crime and fewer victims.

This is the fourth in our series of cookbooks. To create them, we collect recipes from our Charity Ambassadors, Trustees, Employees and supporters, with the entire proceeds of sales going towards continuing our work to reduce crime in the UK. I would like to thank Al Crisci and all our contributors, particularly Alison Cathie and her team, for the beautiful book they've made.

I hope that you enjoy the recipes and, while cooking them, that you will remember how you

are helping inmates to rehabilitate themselves. The very act of food preparation and cooking is restorative for our inmates, and it gives them a skill they can use to re-enter society.

Bon Appétit

Herbs

Mojo verde

This is great with fish, potatoes, roast vegetables, or just as a dip with bread.

Makes enough for 4

Ingredients

1 bunch of coriander
½ bunch of parsley
5 large garlic cloves
2 small green peppers, chopped
1 green chilli, finely chopped
1–2 tsp sea salt
¼ tsp ground cumin, or to taste
240ml good-quality extra virgin olive oil
2 tbsp sherry vinegar, or red wine vinegar, or to taste

Method

• Remove the coarse stems from the coriander and parsley and roughly chop the leaves.
• Roughly chop the garlic and mash it to a paste in a mortar and pestle. Put the coriander, parsley, mashed garlic, peppers, chilli, the smaller amount of salt and the cumin in a blender or food processor and pulse a couple of times.
• Slowly drizzle in the olive oil while blending slowly: you don't want to over-process the sauce, the truly traditional (but tiring!) way would be to do it all in a mortar and pestle.
• Stir in the vinegar to taste, then adjust the salt and cumin. Sealed with a layer of oil, this keeps in the fridge for up to 1 week.

Italian vinaigrette

Makes enough for salad for 4

Ingredients

4 tsp Dijon mustard
juice of 1 large lemon
300ml extra virgin olive oil
2 tsp dried oregano
sea salt and freshly ground black pepper

Method

• Take a 500ml glass jar with a screw lid. Put in the mustard, lemon juice and half the oil, fit the lid on tightly and shake it all together vigorously.
• Remove the lid and add the remaining oil and the oregano, then season to taste. Replace the lid and shake again; the dressing will become thick and emulsified.
• Store in the fridge for up to 1 week.

Clockwise from top: Chimichurri (see page 8); Chilli salsa verde (see page 8), Basil pesto (see page 9); Italian vinaigrette; Mojo verde

Chilli salsa verde

Ellie Shaw, Chef-trainer, Clink Brixton

Great with fish, lamb and vegetables.

Serves 6–8

Ingredients
1 red chilli, seeds left in
2 garlic cloves
1 bunch of flat-leaf parsley
1 bunch of basil
1 bunch of coriander
leaves from 4 mint sprigs
1 large tbsp capers, rinsed and drained
juice of 1 lemon
extra virgin olive oil, as much as you need
freshly ground black pepper

Method
• Put the chilli in a food processor with the garlic, all the herbs, the capers and lemon juice and blend.
• Slowly add olive oil, with the motor running, until you have a thick consistency.
• Season the salsa verde to taste with black pepper.
• Sealed with a layer of oil, this keeps in the fridge for up to 1 week.

Chimichurri

Use this with rare steak and grilled meats

Makes enough for 4

Ingredients
60g flat-leaf parsley leaves
4 garlic cloves, peeled and smashed
15g oregano leaves, or 4 tsp dried oregano

4 tbsp red wine vinegar
½ tsp chilli flakes (optional)
sea salt and freshly ground black pepper
240ml good-quality extra virgin olive oil

Basil pesto

Serves 4 with pasta

Ingredients

120g pine nuts

125g Parmesan cheese (or a
   vegetarian alternative), cut
   into small chunks

leaves from 1 large bunch
   of basil

1 garlic clove, crushed with the
   flat side of a knife

200ml extra virgin olive oil

sea salt and freshly ground
   black pepper

squeeze of lemon juice
   (optional)

Method

• Heat a dry frying pan over a medium heat. Add the pine nuts
and toast them for a few minutes until browned and fragrant.

• Place the Parmesan chunks in a food processor and add the
basil leaves, garlic, toasted pine nuts and olive oil. Season to
taste with salt and pepper. Blend for a few seconds until it comes
together and is smooth.

• Taste for seasoning and add the lemon juice, if you like.

• If not using it immediately, you can store the pesto in a jar,
with a layer of oil to seal it from the air; it will keep for 1 week
in the fridge.

Method

• Place the parsley, garlic, oregano, vinegar, chilli flakes and salt and pepper to taste in a food
processor. Process until finely chopped, stopping and scraping down the sides of the processor
bowl with a rubber spatula as needed. It should take about 1 minute.

• With the motor running, add the olive oil in a steady stream. Scrape down the sides of the bowl
and pulse a few final times to combine.

• Transfer the sauce to an airtight container and refrigerate for at least 2 hours or up to 1 day to
allow the flavours to come together. Before serving, stir, taste and season again as needed. The
chimichurri will keep, sealed with a layer of oil, in the fridge for up to 1 week.

Gravlax with horseradish sauce

Serves 6

Ingredients

FOR THE GRAVLAX

2 x 750g skin-on salmon fillets

1 large bunch of dill, roughly chopped

100g coarse sea salt

75g white sugar (any sort)

2 tbsp coarsely crushed white peppercorns

FOR THE HORSERADISH AND MUSTARD SAUCE

2 tsp finely grated fresh horseradish root

2 tsp finely grated onion

1 tsp Dijon mustard

1 tsp caster sugar

2 tbsp white wine vinegar

good pinch of sea salt

175ml double cream

Method

• Start 2 days ahead of when you want to eat. Put one of the salmon fillets, skin-side down, on a large sheet of cling film. Mix the dill with the salt, sugar and crushed peppercorns and spread it over the salmon. Place the other fillet on top, skin-side up.

• Tightly wrap in 3 or 4 layers of cling film and lift on to a large, shallow tray. Rest a slightly smaller tray or chopping board on top and weigh it down with cans, or a heavy mortar and pestle.

• Refrigerate for 2 days, turning the fish every 12 hours so that the brine mixture that develops inside the cling film parcel bastes the outside of the fish.

• For the sauce, on the day of serving stir together all the ingredients except the cream. Whip the cream to soft peaks, stir in the horseradish mixture, cover and chill.

• Remove the fish from the brine mixture and slice it as you would smoked salmon, then serve with the chilled cream on the side. Provide good sourdough or rye bread.

White bean & garlic soup with wild garlic pesto

Mark Sillery, Clink Director of Mentoring

Serves 4–6

Ingredients

FOR THE SOUP

300g dried white beans
  (haricot or cannellini)
1 bulb of garlic, cloves
  separated, skins left on
600ml whole milk
3 tbsp olive oil
2 leeks, well washed and
  finely chopped
leaves from 1 rosemary sprig,
  finely chopped
2 litres vegetable stock
sea salt and freshly ground
  black pepper
splash of double cream,
  to serve (optional)
garlic flavoured extra virgin
  olive oil, to serve (optional)

FOR THE PESTO

60g pine nuts
2 handfuls (about 75g) wild
  garlic leaves, chopped
4–6 tbsp extra virgin olive oil
3 tbsp finely grated Parmesan
  cheese

Method

• The night before you make the soup, soak the beans in cold water. The next morning, drain them in a colander, then rinse.
• Place the garlic cloves in a saucepan and pour over one-third of the milk. Set over a medium heat and bring to the boil, then discard the milk. Repeat twice more. When the garlic is cool enough to handle, peel and crush the cloves. This process takes the harshness from the garlic and makes it sweet.
• Heat the olive oil in a large, heavy-based saucepan and gently sweat the leeks and rosemary until they soften slightly. Take care not to brown them, to prevent them from becoming bitter.
• Add the beans and stock, bring to the boil and boil rapidly for 10 minutes. Reduce the heat to a steady simmer and cook, uncovered, until the beans are soft; this takes about 45 minutes.
• Add the crushed garlic, then taste and adjust the seasoning.
• Meanwhile, make the pesto. Toast the pine nuts in a dry frying pan until golden brown, then tip into a food processor with the wild garlic, extra virgin olive oil and Parmesan and blitz to a smooth paste. Season to taste, then set aside.
• Carefully pour the soup into a blender – or use a stick blender – and purée until smooth, splashing in a little water if it is too thick. Return to a clean saucepan and reheat gently until hot. Check the seasoning, adding a little salt and pepper if needed.
• For extra richness, add a dash of cream and/or some flavoured extra virgin olive oil when you serve the soup.
• Serve it in warmed bowls with a spoonful of pesto swirled on top, offering the remaining pesto in a bowl on the side.

Omelette aux fines herbes

A classic, but deceptively easy to get wrong! It should be moist inside (not runny) and lightly brown outside (not dry).

Makes 6

Ingredients

18 eggs
sea salt and freshly ground black pepper
2 tbsp chopped chives
2 tbsp chopped chervil leaves
2 tsp chopped parsley leaves
130g unsalted butter

Method

• Break the eggs into a large bowl. Add salt and pepper and the herbs. Beat lightly with a fork to blend. Leave the mixture to rest for at least 30 minutes to allow the herbs to flavour the eggs.

• Heat 15g of the butter in a 15cm omelette pan (preferably non-stick) over a medium heat until bubbling; do not let the butter brown. Pour in about one-sixth of the egg mixture and cook gently, stirring constantly.

• When the eggs begin to set but are still soft on top, use a spatula to fold the edge of the omelette that is closest to the pan handle in towards the centre (ideally fold the omelette into thirds). Lift up the folded edge and slide about 1 tsp more butter under it. Then, with your free hand, tap the handle of the pan sharply, so that the far edge of the omelette slides up the side of the pan. Fold this edge in towards the centre and continue cooking for about 2 minutes, until the omelette is very lightly golden on the bottom.

• Turn the omelette out, seam-side down, on to a plate. If necessary, reshape the omelette into an even form. Pour any butter remaining in the pan over the omelette.

• Serve immediately, while you cook the remaining omelettes in the same way.

Sage butter

Debbie Whitworth, Clink Finance Director

Serves 4 as a pasta sauce

Ingredients

50g unsalted butter
juice of ½ lemon
1–2 tablespoons chopped
   sage leaves

Method

• Melt the butter in a
heavy-based saucepan over
a medium heat until melted
and golden.
• Remove the pan from the
heat, stand back, then
squeeze in the lemon juice.
Add the sage leaves and toss
with drained pasta or gnocchi
to serve.

Tom yum

Ellie Shaw, Chef-trainer, Clink Brixton

Serves 6

Ingredients

4 garlic cloves
2 red chillies, seeds left in
4cm fresh root ginger, peeled
2 lemongrass stalks
4 tbsp olive oil
3 tbsp rice wine vinegar
3 tbsp honey

4 tbsp soy sauce
juice of 2 limes
1.5 litres vegetable stock
200g vermicelli rice noodles
200g beansprouts
200g baby sweetcorn
1 bunch of coriander, chopped

Herby spelt salad

Daniel Ayton, Clink Chef Ambassador

Serves 3–4 as a side dish

Ingredients

120g cooked spelt grains
1 tbsp chopped chives
1 tbsp chopped flat-leaf
   parsley leaves
1 tbsp extra virgin olive oil
1 tsp sherry vinegar
sea salt and freshly ground
   black pepper

Method

• Mix the cooked spelt grains with the herbs, oil and vinegar, season to taste and leave for 10 minutes to develop and round out the flavours.
• Great with salmon fillets, or as a side dish at a barbecue.

Method

• Make a paste – or at least a finely chopped mass – with the garlic, chillies, ginger and lemongrass. This can be done either by chopping them together finely, or by chopping them into a mortar and pestle and working them to a paste Add to a large saucepan with the oil and cook over a low heat for 2 minutes.
• Add the rice wine vinegar, honey, soy sauce and lime juice and cook for a further 2 minutes. Pour in the stock, bring to a simmer and cook for 5 minutes over a medium heat.
• Now add the vermicelli noodles, beansprouts and baby sweetcorn, return to a simmer once again and cook for a final 5 minutes over a medium heat.
• Remove from the heat and sprinkle over the coriander. Serve immediately, in warmed bowls.

Vegetable pho

Serves 4

Ingredients

FOR THE SOUP

1 cinnamon stick

3 cloves

2 star anise

1 large onion, quartered

10cm piece of fresh root
    ginger, peeled and
    halved lengthways

1 litre vegetable stock

2 tbsp tamari sauce, plus
    more to taste (optional)

175g rice noodles

1 tbsp mild extra virgin
    olive oil

150g shiitake mushrooms,
    finely sliced

sea salt

TO GARNISH

mung bean sprouts

basil leaves or sprigs (ideally
    Thai basil), or coriander
    leaves or sprigs

mint leaves or sprigs

spring onion greens,
    finely sliced

green chilli, very finely sliced

lime wedges

Method

• Warm a saucepan over a medium heat. Add the cinnamon stick, cloves and star anise and toast until fragrant (this should take 3–4 minutes), stirring occasionally. Add the onion, ginger, vegetable stock, 1 litre of water and the tamari. Increase the heat to high and bring to the boil, then reduce the heat to a gentle simmer and cook gently for 30 minutes, to give all the flavours time to develop.

• Meanwhile, prepare the rice noodles according to the packet instructions and refresh in cold water. Set aside.

• Warm the olive oil in a saucepan over a medium heat until fairly hot. Add the mushrooms and a few pinches of salt. Cook until the mushrooms are tender and lightly browned, which should take 4–6 minutes, then set aside.

• Once the broth is ready, strain it into a large bowl. Season to taste, adding more tamari sauce, or salt, if you want. Ladle the broth into warmed bowls and add the cooked noodles and mushrooms.

• Now, add fresh garnishes to your heart's content (don't forget the lime!). Serve immediately, with chopsticks and soup spoons.

Shoots

Raw fennel, kohlrabi & orange salad with saffron

Daniel Ayton, Clink Chef Ambassador

Serves 4 as a starter or side dish

Ingredients

FOR THE SAFFRON-ORANGE VINAIGRETTE

2 tbsp extra virgin olive oil
pinch of saffron threads
120ml orange juice, preferably freshly squeezed

FOR THE SALAD

1 fennel bulb
1 head of kohlrabi
1 small head of white chicory
finely grated zest and separated segments of 2 oranges
1 tbsp chopped dill, plus more to serve
sea salt and freshly ground black pepper

Method

• Start with the vinaigrette. In a small saucepan, gently heat the olive oil, then crumble over the saffron. Remove from the heat and leave to stand for 10 minutes. Add the orange juice, place over a medium-high heat and boil to reduce by half. Leave to cool completely.
• Remove the outer layer from the fennel bulb and use a sharp mandolin to finely shave the fennel into a large mixing bowl. Peel the kohlrabi and finely slice using the mandolin, then finely julienne with a sharp knife. Add it to the fennel. Wash the chicory, remove the root end and separate the leaves, then add the chicory to the fennel mixture.
• Add the orange zest, orange segments and chopped dill and season to taste. Toss through the cooled vinaigrette, then serve sprinkled with a little more dill.

Asparagus risotto

Jason Swettenham, HM Prison Service

Serves 4–6

Ingredients

2 bunches of asparagus,
  woody ends removed
1.7 litres vegetable or
  chicken stock
2 tbsp olive oil
1 large onion, finely chopped
4–5 celery stalks, finely
  chopped
600g risotto rice
250ml vermouth or
  dry white wine
50g unsalted butter
1 small handful of finely grated
  Parmesan cheese,
  plus more to serve
leaves from 1 bunch of mint,
  finely chopped
finely grated zest and juice of
  2 unwaxed lemons
sea salt and freshly ground
  black pepper
extra virgin olive oil, to serve

Method

• Finely chop the asparagus stalks, keeping the tips whole.
• Bring 1 litre of the stock to a simmer in a saucepan. Put the olive oil in a separate large pan, add the onion and celery and cook gently for about 15 minutes, without colouring, until soft. Add the rice (it will sizzle) and increase the heat. Don't let the rice or veg catch on the pan, keep it moving.
• Quickly pour in the vermouth or wine. Keep stirring all the time until it has evaporated, leaving the rice with a lovely perfume.
• Add the stock a ladle at a time, stirring and waiting until each ladleful has been fully absorbed before adding the next. Reduce the heat to low so the rice doesn't cook too quickly, otherwise the outside of each grain will be stodgy and the inside hard and nutty; you don't want to cook it too slowly either, or it will turn into rice pudding! Continue to add ladlefuls of stock until it has all been absorbed. This should take 14–15 minutes and give you rice that is beginning to soften but is still a little al dente.
• Put a large saucepan over a medium-high heat and pour in 350ml of stock, followed by all the risotto and the asparagus stalks and tips. Stirring all the time, gently bring to the boil, then reduce the heat and simmer until almost all the stock has been absorbed. Add the rest of the stock a ladleful at a time until the rice and asparagus are cooked. You might not need it all. Be careful not to overcook the rice: keep making sure it's a pleasure to eat. It should hold its shape but be soft, creamy and oozy, and the texture should be slightly looser than you think you want it.
• Turn off the heat, beat in the butter and Parmesan, mint, almost all the lemon zest and all the juice. Check the seasoning. Put a lid on the pan and leave to rest for 1 minute. Serve with a drizzle of extra virgin olive oil, a scattering of the remaining lemon zest and a block of Parmesan on the table.

Big Pete's baba ganoush

Peter Thomas, Clink Friend, 06:03:54–18:06:18

Serves 8–10 as a dip

Ingredients
4 large aubergines
3 garlic cloves
½ tsp sea salt
3 tbsp lemon juice, or to taste
3 tbsp tahini
large pinch of ground cumin
pinch of freshly ground black pepper
1 heaped tbsp low-fat sour cream
2 tbsp low-fat crème fraîche
extra virgin olive oil, to serve
chopped flat-leaf parsley leaves, to serve

Method
• Preheat the grill. Prick the aubergines with a fork and grill them, turning occasionally, until the skin blisters and blackens all over; it should be charred and brittle.
• Leave to cool, then cut each aubergine in half and scoop out the flesh with a spoon. Leave it in a colander for 20 minutes, to drain off the excess liquid.
• Pound the garlic and salt until smooth in a mortar and pestle. Transfer to a food processor and add the drained aubergine flesh, lemon juice, tahini, cumin, pepper, sour cream and crème fraîche. Whizz to a thick purée.
• Adjust the seasoning and add more lemon juice if needed. Spoon into a bowl, drizzle with extra virgin olive oil, sprinkle with parsley and serve.

Moroccan pumpkin & chestnut soup

Daniel Ayton, Clink Chef Ambassador

Serves 4

Ingredients

100g unsalted butter

1kg pumpkin, peeled, deseeded and chopped

1 tbsp ras el hanout

1 tsp each ground cumin and chilli flakes

200ml dry white wine

1.2 litres chicken or vegetable stock

100g cooked and peeled chestnuts

80g Parmesan cheese, finely grated

squeeze of lemon juice (optional)

Method

• Preheat the oven to 200°C (Gas 6).

• Melt the butter, add the pumpkin, spices, salt and pepper. When the pumpkin colours, stir in the wine until absorbed, then the stock. Bring to a simmer and cook for 20 minutes.

• Chop half the chestnuts and spread on a baking tray. Cook in the oven until toasted.

• Add the cheese and unroasted chestnuts to the soup and cook for 10 minutes.

• Blend until smooth. Taste and add lemon juice if you want. Reheat gently and serve with the toasted chestnuts.

Minestrone

Sally Scott, Clink Friend

Serves 4

Ingredients

1 litre vegetable stock

6 plum tomatoes, chopped

1 tbsp basil leaves, chopped

½ tsp oregano leaves, chopped

2 carrots, finely chopped

2 celery stalks, finely sliced

½ onion, finely chopped

3 small courgettes, finely chopped

125g green beans, cut into short lengths

3 garlic cloves, finely chopped

1 bay leaf

sea salt and freshly ground black pepper

150g orzo

handful of chopped parsley leaves

Parmesan cheese, finely grated, to serve

Method

• Pour the stock into a large pot, then add the tomatoes, basil, oregano, carrots, celery, onion, courgettes, green beans, garlic and bay.

• Slowly bring the soup to a low simmer and cook over a very low heat for 30–45 minutes, or until the vegetables are tender, stirring from time to time. Add salt and pepper and the orzo and increase the heat to medium. Allow to simmer for another 10 minutes, or until the pasta is cooked.

• Remove the bay leaf, then serve sprinkled with the parsley and Parmesan.

Goat's cheese towers

Christopher Moore, Clink Chief Executive

Serves 4 as a substantial starter or light lunch

Ingredients

1 small ciabatta loaf, cut into
    8 x 1cm-thick slices
jar of green pesto
2 beef tomatoes, each cut into
    1cm-thick slices
1 goat's cheese log, cut into
    1cm-thick slices
4 sprigs of rosemary, each
    10cm long
bottle of balsamic syrup
small bag of rocket

Method

• Preheat the oven to 120°C (Gas ½).
• Lightly toast the ciabatta on both sides. Lightly spread 1 side of each piece with pesto. Lay out in pairs on a baking sheet.
• Place the tomato slices on each piece, then stack 2 slices for each serving. Place the goat's cheese slices on top. Skewer each tower with a cocktail stick to secure while cooking.
• Bake in the oven for 10 minutes, then slide under a preheated grill until the cheese is brown (not melting).
• Take each rosemary sprig, strip the first 6cm, then remove the cocktail stick from each tower and replace it with a sprig.
• Zigzag the balsamic syrup on 4 plates. Place the towers on the plates with a handful of rocket.

Asparagus tartlets

Jane Sanderson, Clink Director of Operations & Training

Makes 6

Ingredients

115g plain flour, plus more to dust
90g unsalted butter, chopped
225g thin asparagus spears, the fresher the better
8 eggs
4 tbsp milk
sea salt and freshly ground black pepper

Method

• You will need six 10cm tartlet tins.
• Preheat the oven to 200°C (Gas 6).
• Sift the flour into a bowl. Rub in three-quarters of the butter until the mixture resembles crumbs. Now stir in enough water to make a soft dough.
• Roll the pastry out on a flour-dusted work top and use it to line the tartlet tins. Prick the bases of the pastry and chill for about 10 minutes.
• Line the tartlet tins with baking parchment and baking beans and bake blind for 10 minutes. Remove the paper and the beans and bake for a further 5–10 minutes, or until the pastry looks lightly golden and cooked.
• Cook the asparagus in boiling water until just tender (the time this takes will depend on its thickness, but start checking after 4 minutes). Drain and leave to cool slightly. Cut off and reserve the tips, then finely chop the rest of the stalks.
• Beat together the eggs, milk and seasoning in a jug.
• Heat the remaining butter in a small pan, add the egg mixture and cook over a low heat until just setting. Stir in the finely chopped asparagus and spoon into the hot pastry cases. Top with the reserved asparagus tips and serve at once.

Kale & chicken Caesar salad

Dan Snow, TV presenter & Clink Ambassador

Serves 1

Ingredients

100g kale, coarse stalks removed

50g spring greens, coarse stalks removed

3 tbsp good-quality ready-made honey and mustard dressing

100g cooked chicken, shredded

4 salted anchovies, chopped

1 tbsp finely grated Parmesan cheese

1 tbsp chopped chives

Method

• Shred the kale and spring greens finely.

• Toss the greens with the dressing.

• Top with all the other ingredients to serve.

Crispy aubergine & courgette antipasto

Serves 6 as a nibble

Ingredients

flavourless vegetable oil, to fry

sea salt and freshly ground black pepper

2 large aubergines, cut lengthways into 5mm slices

3 courgettes, cut lengthways into 5mm slices

75ml extra virgin olive oil

3 garlic cloves, finely chopped

juice of ½ lemon, plus lemon wedges to serve (optional)

leaves from 1 bunch of mint, finely chopped

Method

• Take a large, heavy-based frying pan and fill it 5mm deep with vegetable oil. Place it over a medium heat.

• Season the aubergine and courgette slices well.

• Once the oil is hot, cook the vegetables a few at a time, turning once with a slotted spoon. Once golden on both sides, remove with the slotted spoon and place on a plate lined with kitchen paper to blot off excess oil.

• Once cooked and drained, place on a large platter, alternating slices of aubergine and courgette and twisting them slightly, if possible, to create movement.

• Mix the extra virgin olive oil, garlic, lemon juice and mint in a bowl. Pour this dressing over the vegetables while they are still warm and season with a little salt. Serve immediately, with lemon wedges for squeezing, if you like.

Roasted vegetable & quinoa salad

Christa Janse van Rensburg, Head Chef Trainer, Clink Events

Serves 4

Ingredients

400g peeled, deseeded and chopped summer squash

50ml olive oil

1 red chilli, deseeded and finely chopped

2 garlic cloves, peeled but left whole

200g peas, frozen are fine

200g Tenderstem broccoli

2 bunches of asparagus

200g cooked black quinoa

200g cooked white quinoa

large handful of chopped flat-leaf parsley leaves

finely grated zest and juice of 2 unwaxed lemons

sea salt and freshly ground black pepper

Method

• Preheat the oven to 220°C (Gas 7).

• Toss the squash on a baking tray with 15ml of the olive oil, the chilli and garlic, then roast for about 20 minutes, or until the squash has a nice colour and is tender. Set aside to cool.

• Bring a saucepan of water to the boil. Drop in the peas, cook for 2 minutes, then remove with a slotted spoon and plunge into iced water. Do the same for the broccoli florets and asparagus spears. Drain all the vegetables and dry with a clean tea towel.

• Heat a griddle pan over a high heat until very hot. Brush the broccoli and asparagus with half the remaining oil and grill them on the griddle pan so they get a nice grilled and smoky flavour and are marked with griddle lines. Leave to cool.

• Mix all the vegetables with the quinoa.

• Stir in the parsley, lemon zest and juice and remaining oil and season with salt and pepper.

Roasted cauliflower salad with olives, capers & parsley

Healthy, gluten-free, vegetarian and packed with flavour. Good either as a salad or as a hot dish.

Hamish Boden, Clink Friend

Ingredients

olive oil

1 large (1kg) cauliflower

sea salt and freshly ground
   black pepper

15g flat-leaf parsley leaves

3 tbsp capers, drained and
   rinsed

80g pitted black olives

45g finely grated pecorino
   cheese

juice and finely grated zest of
   ½ unwaxed lemon

extra virgin olive oil, to serve

Method

• Preheat the oven to 200°C (Gas 6). Put a good glug of olive oil in a baking tray and put it in the oven to heat up.

• Remove the leaves from the cauliflower and set aside. Remove the stalk, then chop the cauliflower into small florets. Spread the florets on the baking tray and season, then roast for 30 minutes, tossing several times during cooking. Place in a large bowl.

• If preparing for later, let the cauliflower cool before adding the remaining ingredients, to maximise freshness. Otherwise prepare the other ingredients now.

• Finely chop the parsley, capers and olives and toss into the cauliflower, adding the pecorino.

• Add the lemon juice and zest with a drizzle of extra virgin olive oil and season to taste.

Orecchiette with turnip tops & chilli

Giorgio Locatelli, Clink Chef Ambassador

Serves 4

Ingredients

3 small bunches of turnip tops (cime di rapa)
sea salt and freshly ground black pepper
5 tbsp extra virgin olive oil
2 garlic cloves, thinly sliced
2 medium red chillies, deseeded (leave the seeds in if you want more heat) and finely sliced
400g dried orecchiette
2 anchovy fillets

Method

• Take the leaves and florets of the turnip tops from their stalks and blanch them in boiling salted water for about 1 minute, just to take away some of their bitterness. Drain and squeeze, to remove the excess water. Chop very finely.
• Warm half the olive oil in a large sauté pan, add the garlic and chillies and gently cook without allowing them to colour. Then add the turnip tops and toss around. Add another 1 tbsp of olive oil.
• Meanwhile, bring a large pan of salted water to the boil, add the orecchiette and cook for about 1 minute less than the time given on the packet (usually 10–12 minutes), until al dente.
• While the pasta is cooking, ladle out a little of the cooking water, add to the pan containing the turnip tops, reduce the heat, then add the anchovies. Let them dissolve, without frying them, stirring all the time. Taste and season, remembering that the anchovies will add saltiness.
• When the pasta is cooked, drain – reserving the cooking water – and add the pasta to the pan containing the sauce. Toss around for 2–3 minutes, so that the turnip tops cook a little more and begin to cling to the pasta, adding splashes of the pasta cooking water if needed. Add the rest of the olive oil, toss through well and serve.

Cauliflower dauphinoise

David & Wendy Ayton, Clink Friends

Serves 6–8 as a side dish

Ingredients

sea salt and freshly ground black pepper
1 cauliflower, cut into florets
600ml double cream
1 garlic clove, finely chopped
a little unsalted butter
freshly grated nutmeg
2 large handfuls of grated Gruyère or Cheddar cheese

Method

• Preheat the oven to 180°C (Gas 4). Bring a large saucepan of salted water to the boil.
• Finely slice the cauliflower florets and blanch for 1 minute in the salted water. Drain well.
• Meanwhile, heat the cream with the garlic in a separate saucepan. Butter a medium ovenproof dish well.
• Place one-third of the cauliflower in the prepared dish, cover with one-third of the cream, then season with black pepper and nutmeg. Add one-third of the grated cheese. Add another layer of cauliflower, cream, seasoning and cheese, then make a third layer, again finishing with the cheese. Bake for 45 minutes.
• Leave to rest for 10 minutes, then serve.

Cauliflower pakoras

Paul Crewe, Clink Data & Compliance Manager

Serves 4 as a starter

Ingredients

200g plain flour

100g gram flour, plus more to dust

½ tsp garam masala

½ tsp chilli flakes

½ tsp ground turmeric

sea salt

50g spinach leaves, chopped

large handful of coriander leaves, chopped

½ cauliflower, cut into small florets

flavourless vegetable oil, to deep-fry

Method

• Mix the flours, spices and salt to taste together in a large bowl, then add 150ml of water and mix to a very thick batter. Stir in the spinach and coriander.

• Bring a large saucepan of water to the boil and place a large bowl of iced water in the kitchen sink. Drop the cauliflower florets into the saucepan and blanch for 1 minute, then drain and plunge straight into the iced water. Drain very well.

• Place a large saucepan over a medium heat and fill it no deeper than one-third full with vegetable oil. Wait until it is hot. If you have a cooking thermometer, it should read 180°C. Otherwise, throw in a drop of batter: if it sizzles immediately, the oil is ready.

• Dust the cauliflower florets in gram flour and dip them in the batter. Fry a few at a time, in batches, for around 2 minutes, then turn with a slotted spoon and fry for another 2 minutes. Lift out with the slotted spoon, place on kitchen paper to blot off any excess oil, season generously with salt, then serve. These are lovely with minted yogurt and / or mango chutney.

Brussels sprouts thoran

Cyrus Todiwala, Clink Chef Ambassador

Serves 4 as part of a spread

Ingredients

1 tbsp vegetable oil

1 tsp black mustard seeds

½ tsp cumin seeds

10–12 curry leaves, finely sliced

2 green chillies, finely chopped

1 tsp finely chopped fresh root ginger

¼ tsp asafoetida

1 small onion, roughly chopped

2–3 tbsp grated fresh coconut

10–12 Brussels sprouts, shredded

1 tbsp finely chopped coriander leaves

Method

• Heat the oil in a frying pan and add the mustard and cumin seeds. Cook until they begin to pop, then add the curry leaves, chillies, ginger and asafoetida. Stir for a few seconds, then add the onion and coconut, stirring until the coconut gives off a nutty aroma.

• Add the Brussels sprouts, cover tightly with a lid and cook for 1–2 minutes. Take off the lid and cook for 2 minutes, stirring occasionally, until dry. Stir through the coriander and serve.

Chinese-style cabbage stir-fry

Serves 4 as a side dish

Ingredients

1 tsp toasted sesame oil
5 garlic cloves, finely chopped
250g cabbage, chopped
¼ tsp vegetable bouillon
   powder
½ tsp chilli flakes
dash of soy sauce
2 tsp sesame seeds

Method

• Heat the sesame oil, add the garlic and brown slightly. Add the cabbage and bouillon, chilli flakes and soy and stir for 2 minutes.
• Sprinkle with the sesame seeds and serve.

Stir-fried Brussels sprouts

Duncan Bell, Clink Friend

Serves 4 as a side dish

Ingredients

1 tbsp toasted sesame oil,
   or vegetable oil
325g Brussels sprouts,
   trimmed and quartered
   lengthways
small handful of sultanas
generous dash of soy sauce
1–2cm fresh root ginger,
   peeled and finely grated

Method

• Heat the oil in a wok over a medium-high heat. Add the sprouts and stir-fry for a few minutes until the outsides soften slightly. Add the sultanas and keep stirring.
• Stir in the soy sauce and ginger and serve immediately.

Grilled halloumi & peach salad

Thomasina Miers, Clink Chef Ambassador

Serves 4–6

Ingredients

6 small courgettes, peeled into strips with a vegetable peeler
  (discard the seedy centres)
4 peaches, cut into thick wedges
big handful of mint leaves, roughly chopped
juice of 1 large lemon, plus more to taste
4 tbsp extra virgin olive oil, plus more to taste
20g unsalted butter
sea salt and freshly ground black pepper
50g skin-on almonds, roughly chopped
¼ tsp smoked paprika
500g halloumi, cut into 1cm-thick slices

Method

• Put the courgette ribbons in a bowl with the peaches, mint, lemon juice and 3 tbsp of the olive oil. Toss well.

• Place a small frying pan over a medium heat, add the butter and season generously. Swirl continuously until the butter starts darkening, then add the almonds and paprika and cook until the butter is a biscuit colour and the almonds are golden. Scatter over the salad.

• Rub the halloumi with the remaining oil, then griddle on a scorching-hot griddle pan for 30–60 seconds on each side, until charred and softened. Cut each piece in half, toss into the salad, then taste and see if you want more black pepper, lemon juice or oil. Season and serve immediately.

Gazpacho

Daniel Ayton, Clink Chef Ambassador

Serves 6–8

Ingredients

FOR THE SOUP

2 thick slices of good sourdough bread, left to go stale, crusts cut off

1.25kg ripe tomatoes, peeled and deseeded

½ onion, roughly chopped

½ cucumber, peeled, deseeded and roughly chopped

½ green pepper, roughly chopped

240ml good-quality extra virgin olive oil

4 tsp sherry vinegar

3 ice cubes

TO SERVE

finely chopped peeled and deseeded tomato

finely chopped green pepper

finely chopped deseeded cucumber

croutons (optional)

Method

• Tear up the bread and place it in a bowl. Pour over water to just cover and set aside for about 20 minutes. Squeeze the excess water out of the bread and place it in a blender.

• Put the tomatoes, onion, cucumber and green pepper into the blender and process until smooth, adding the olive oil and half the vinegar.

• Now push the gazpacho through a sieve. This will get rid of any remaining tomato seeds or skin or any other lumps. Taste and add the remaining vinegar if you want. It should taste sharp. If it seems too thick, add water to get a consistency that you prefer.

• Pour the gazpacho into a serving bowl, add the ice cubes and put it all in the fridge to chill.

• Put the finely chopped tomato, green pepper, cucumber and croutons, if using, into small bowls and serve with the chilled gazpacho.

Feta & pepper empanadillas

Makes about 20

Ingredients

FOR THE DOUGH

120ml olive oil, plus more for
the baking sheet

120ml dry white wine, or water

½ tsp fine sea salt

300g plain flour, plus more
to dust

2 large egg yolks, lightly
beaten with 1 tsp water

FOR THE FILLING

½ large onion, finely chopped

2 tbsp olive oil

3 tomatoes, peeled and
chopped

sea salt and freshly ground
black pepper

1 roasted red pepper, peeled,
deseeded and chopped

14 green or black olives, pitted
and chopped

2 tbsp chopped flat-leaf
parsley leaves

115g feta cheese, finely
chopped or crumbled

Method

• Start with the dough. Mix the olive oil, wine or water and salt
in a bowl, beating with a fork. Gradually work in enough flour to
make a soft, smooth, malleable dough that does not stick to the
bowl or to your hands; begin by stirring the flour in with a fork,
then work it in with your hands and knead briefly. You can use
the dough now or keep it for up to 1 day, wrapped in cling film at
room temperature, not in the fridge.

• To make the filling, fry the onion in the olive oil in a large frying
pan until very soft, stirring often. Add the tomatoes and cook
over a medium heat until the liquid has disappeared and you can
see the oil sizzling. Season to taste. Add the red pepper, olives
and parsley. Mix well, then leave to cool. Add the feta when cool.

• Preheat the oven to 180°C (Gas 4).

• To assemble the empanadillas, divide the dough into 4–6
pieces (it is easier to roll out small amounts). Roll each piece out
as thinly as you can on a well-floured surface and cut into rounds
with a 10cm pastry cutter or a small saucer; you do not need to
flour the surface or the rolling pin, as the dough is oily and will
not stick. Reserve the scraps and roll them into a ball, then roll
out again and cut into rounds; do not waste any dough.

• Fill each batch of pastry rounds as you cut them: brush the
edges with some egg yolk, put a generous 1 tbsp of filling in the
middle, bring 2 opposite sides of the pastry up to meet over the
filling, making a half-moon-shaped pie, pinch the edges together,
then press the seams with the tines of a fork to seal.

• Place the empanadillas on a baking sheet lined with lightly
oiled foil. Brush the tops with the remaining egg yolk and bake
for 30 minutes.

Nordic kale, apple & quinoa salad

Daniel Ayton, Clink Chef Ambassador

Serves 4

Ingredients

FOR THE SALAD

190g red quinoa

50g walnut halves

2 dessert apples, such as Cox

100g kale, coarse stalks removed, leaves shredded

100g red cabbage, shredded

1 celery stalk, finely sliced

FOR THE DRESSING

1 tbsp Dijon mustard

1 tbsp honey

4 tbsp apple cider vinegar

2 tbsp walnut oil

sea salt and freshly ground black pepper

Method

• Cook the quinoa in plenty of boiling water for 15 minutes, or until cooked, then drain well and leave to cool before transferring to a big salad bowl.

• Toast the walnut halves in a dry frying pan for a few minutes, then chop. Allow to cool.

• Finely slice the apples, then mix all the salad ingredients into the salad bowl (the best way to do this is with your hands).

• To make the dressing, whisk together the mustard, honey and vinegar, then whisk in the walnut oil gradually and season to taste. Mix the salad with the dressing just before serving.

Chicory, walnut & Roquefort salad

Natasha Morgan, Clink Friend

Serves 4

Ingredients

4 heads of chicory heads
    (a mixture of green and
    red looks pretty), or even
    blanched green beans
100g Roquefort, crumbled
50g walnuts
juice of ½ lemon
2 tbsp walnut oil

Method

• Throw the chicory or green beans into a large salad bowl and
mix with the Roquefort and walnuts.
• Stir in the lemon juice and walnut oil and serve.

Sweetcorn, caper & pine nut salad

Debbie Whitworth, Clink Finance Director

Serves 4

Ingredients

30g sultanas
4 sweetcorn cobs, or 200g
    cooked sweetcorn kernels
20g unsalted butter
30g pine nuts
juice of ½ lemon
2–3 tablespoons capers,
    rinsed and drained
1 tsp thyme leaves

Method

• Soak the sultanas in hot water for 2 hours.
• Meanwhile, boil the sweetcorn cobs, if using, for 10 minutes,
then drain. When cool enough to handle, stand each cob on its
end and slice off the kernels with a sharp knife.
• Melt the butter in a heavy-based saucepan over a medium heat
and wait until it is a slightly golden colour with a light toasty
aroma, then add the pine nuts and stir until golden. Add the
lemon juice, sweetcorn, drained sultanas, capers and thyme,
then serve.

Artichoke, melted onion & Brie tart

Matt Tebbutt, Clink Chef Ambassador

Serves 6–8

Ingredients

FOR THE TART

12 small artichokes

a few bay leaves

sea salt and freshly ground black pepper

6 onions, thickly sliced

2 garlic cloves, sliced

30g unsalted butter

small pack of thyme

400g all-butter puff pastry

150g good-quality Brie cheese

FOR THE VINAIGRETTE

1 tsp Dijon mustard

100ml walnut oil

30ml red wine vinegar

1 garlic clove, crushed, grated
  or very finely chopped

Method

• Bring a large saucepan of water to the boil. Plunge in the artichokes and bay leaves and add some salt. Cover and simmer for 10–15 minutes, or until the thickest part of the artichoke stems are tender. (Insert a cocktail stick to check.) Remove and allow to cool.

• Slice off the top one-third of each artichoke with a serrated knife, pull off the dark outer leaves, leaving the soft lighter ones exposed, then cut vertically through the centre of the artichoke. If necessary (and it's not always), pull out any purple-looking spikes or hairs… this is the 'choke' and you don't want to be eating it! Now cut each in half again and set aside.

• Throw the onions and garlic into a pan with the butter and most of the thyme and stew very gently, without colour, for 1 hour. This is best achieved by covering with a wet piece of scrunched-up then smoothed-out baking parchment and a heavy lid. Check from time to time and stir, so they cook evenly. Season, then tip into a colander to drain. Preheat the oven to 180°C (Gas 4).

• Roll out the pastry into a 30cm round and prick all over, leaving a 1cm rim. Bake for 15–20 minutes until cooked and golden. Whisk the vinaigrette ingredients together, then season.

• When ready to assemble, spoon the onions into the pastry case, scatter in the artichokes and tear in the Brie. Return to the oven for a short time, to reheat everything and melt the cheese.

• Scatter over a few more thyme leaves, dress with the vinaigrette and serve with a green salad.

Hearty breakfast shakshuka

Rebecca Scott, Clink Friend

Serves 4

Ingredients

1 tbsp olive oil

4 spring onions, chopped

½ tsp cumin seeds

½ tsp ground cumin

1 tsp smoked paprika

150g cherry tomatoes, chopped

400g can of chopped tomatoes

sea salt and freshly ground black pepper

pinch of caster sugar

handful of spinach leaves

4 eggs

handful of grated Cheddar cheese

80g crème fraîche

finely chopped chilli, to serve

coriander sprigs, to serve

Method

• Heat the oil in a large, shallow oven- and flameproof pan, then fry the spring onions until aromatic and slightly tender. Add the spices and fresh and canned tomatoes, season to taste and add the sugar to balance the acidity. Gently simmer until the tomatoes soften. Preheat the grill to high.

• Add the spinach to the tomato pan and cook, stirring, until it wilts.

• Create 4 wells in the sauce and crack an egg into each. Gently cook for a few minutes.

• Sprinkle over the Cheddar and dollop on the crème fraîche. Finish cooking the eggs under the hot grill for a few minutes.

• Once the eggs are cooked to your liking, take them straight to the table and sprinkle with chilli and coriander, to taste. Serve with crunchy sourdough toast.

Dutch baby with Roquefort & figs

Somewhere in the middle of the savoury-sweet axis, this is a good light lunch to share, or a Sunday lunch for a vegetarian, or even a 'cheese course'.

Matt Tebbutt, Clink Chef Ambassador

Serves 2

Ingredients

FOR THE BATTER

125g plain flour

125ml whole milk

3 eggs

pinch of ground cinnamon

30g salted butter

FOR THE FILLING

25g salted butter

6–8 black figs (if available, otherwise green), halved

a few thyme sprigs

150g Roquefort cheese

2 tsp runny honey

2 tbsp toasted flaked almonds

Method

• Preheat the oven to 200°C (Gas 6).

• Make the batter by whisking all the ingredients, except the butter, together in a mixing bowl. Place a cast-iron ovenproof pan over a medium-high heat. When it is hot, add the butter, swirl around to coat, then pour in the batter. Bake in the oven for 20 minutes.

• Meanwhile, make the filling. Melt the butter in a frying pan over a medium-high heat and add the figs and thyme. Cook, turning only once the figs have caramelised.

• Remove the batter pudding from the oven, fill it with the caramelised figs and thyme, dot with the Roquefort and serve drizzled with the honey and scattered with the almonds.

Roots

Parisienne gnocchi gratin

HRH The Duchess of Cornwall

Serves 4

Ingredients

50g unsalted butter,
  or margarine
60g plain or wholemeal flour
1 egg, lightly beaten
sea salt
50g grated cheese
1 tbsp extra virgin olive oil
800g spinach, blanched for
  1 minute, excess water
  squeezed out
handful of cherry plum
  tomatoes
300g peas, blanched for
  1 minute, then drained
150g ceps, sliced
250ml thin béchamel sauce
Parmesan cheese, to finish

Method

• Heat 125ml of water and the butter in a saucepan until the butter has melted. Add the flour and beat over a low heat for 4–5 minutes. Remove from the heat and beat in the egg, a little at a time. Season with salt and add the grated cheese.
• Bring a separate saucepan of water to a simmer and have ready a large bowl of iced water. Preheat the oven to 180°C (Gas 4).
• Place the flour mixture into a piping bag fitted with a medium nozzle, then pipe the mixture slowly into the pan of simmering water, using a knife to cut the mixture off at 2cm intervals whilst piping. Poach the gnocchi for 4–5 minutes. They should float to the surface once they are cooked. Scoop them out and place in the iced water to cool. Once cool, drain, then drizzle with the extra virgin olive oil.
• Start to build the gratin in a medium-sized ovenproof dish. Layer the gnocchi with the spinach, tomatoes, peas and ceps. Cover evenly with a layer of the béchamel sauce and sprinkle with the Parmesan.
• Bake for 35–40 minutes, until piping hot and golden brown.

Beetroot hummus

Natasha Morgan, Clink Friend

Serves 4 as a dip

Ingredients

1 raw beetroot, peeled and chopped

400g can of chickpeas, drained and rinsed

2 tsp ground cumin

2 tbsp tahini

100ml olive oil

1 garlic clove, roughly chopped

juice and finely grated zest of 1 unwaxed lemon

handful of flat-leaf parsley leaves

Method

• Put all the ingredients, except the parsley, in a blender and process until smooth.

• Scrape into a bowl, sprinkle with the parsley and serve with warm flatbreads.

Beetroot gratin with horseradish & orange

David & Wendy Ayton, Clink Friends

Ingredients

500g raw beetroots

thick béchamel sauce

3 tbsp double cream

1–2 tbsp creamed horseradish sauce, to taste

finely grated zest and juice of 1 orange

handful of chopped parsley leaves

finely grated Parmesan cheese

Serves 4

Method

• Preheat the oven to 180°C (Gas 4). Wrap the beetroots in foil and bake them for 1 hour, or until tender (a sharp knife should pass right through with no resistance). Leave until cool enough to handle, then chop finely.

• Meanwhile prepare a thick béchamel sauce and add the cream, horseradish and orange zest and juice.

• Combine all together and bake until browned on top (about 20 minutes). Serve topped with a little parsley and scattered with Parmesan cheese.

Roots salad with oranges, feta & pistachio dressing

Lady Edwina Grosvenor, Clink Founder Trustee

Serves 4

Ingredients

FOR THE SALAD

300g beetroots, peeled

5 carrots, peeled

1 small mooli, peeled

6 radishes

100g watercress

2 oranges, segmented

70g feta cheese, crumbled

2 tbsp chopped mint leaves

1 tbsp chopped dill

FOR THE DRESSING

100g pistachios, chopped

finely grated zest and juice
   of 1 orange

1 red chilli, finely chopped

1 garlic clove, crushed

2 tbsp Quick-pickled
   red onions (see right)

3 tbsp extra virgin olive oil

1 tsp balsamic vinegar

sea salt and freshly ground
   black pepper

Method

• Shave all the root veggies using a potato peeler, so you get colourful ribbons. Place them in a mixing bowl.

• Separately mix together all the dressing ingredients, season well, then toss with the vegetables. Taste and season again.

• Put the watercress on a platter and arrange the vegetables on top. Finish with the orange segments, feta and herbs.

QUICK-PICKLED RED ONIONS

3 red onions, sliced into rings

300ml cider vinegar

3 tbsp caster sugar

1 tbsp sea salt

6 black peppercorns

6 coriander seeds

1 star anise

1 bay leaf

• Place the onion rings in a colander and pour over just-boiled water from a full kettle. Leave to drain, still in the colander.

• Pour the vinegar into a saucepan with the sugar, salt, spices and bay. Place over a high heat and bring to a simmer, stirring to dissolve the sugar and salt. Cook for just 1 minute.

• Pack the onion rings into a 500g sterilised jar (see page 100), pour over the warm vinegar and seal. Leave to pickle for a minimum of 2 hours. These keep for 6 months unopened. Once opened, keep in the fridge and eat within 2 weeks.

Celeriac rémoulade

Debbie Whitworth, Clink Finance Director

Serves 4–6 as a side dish

Ingredients
1 medium celeriac
juice of 1 lemon
sea salt
200g mayonnaise
2 tbsp creamed horseradish sauce

Method
• Peel the celeriac and cut it into even, thin slices, each about 3mm thick (a mandolin will help with this). Then cut it into strips 3mm wide to create julienned ribbons.
• Put the celeriac ribbons into a bowl, add the lemon juice and a pinch of salt and mix well. Tip it into a sieve and leave for 1 hour. Bundle up the celeriac in a clean tea towel, then squeeze out any excess liquid.
• Place the celeriac in a bowl and stir in the mayonnaise and horseradish to bind. This is a great side dish to almost anything, but especially good with ham, cheese or terrines.

Potato pizza base

This is a good gluten-free pizza.

Makes 1 / Serves 4

Ingredients

olive oil, for the dish

1.5kg cooked mashed potato

8 medium egg yolks

75g cornflour

50g grated Parmesan cheese

8 basil leaves, plus more to serve

400g tomato passata

100g buffalo mozzarella

Method

• Preheat the oven to 180°C (Gas 4). Brush a 25cm deep pan pizza dish with a little oil.

• Mix the potato, egg yolks and cornflour in a bowl. Add half the Parmesan and beat it in.

• Put the mixture into the pizza dish and push down to the edges to an even thickness.

• Bake in the oven for up to 30 minutes, or until slightly crispy and just beginning to turn golden. Remove from the oven and allow to cool.

• Tear the basil leaves and mix into the passata. Spread the passata evenly over the potato pizza base, leaving a 2cm gap around the edge. Cut the mozzarella into 12 pieces and distribute on top. Sprinkle the remaining Parmesan over the pizza.

• Bake for 12 minutes, then serve, sprinkled with basil leaves.

Sunday lunch frittata

Debbie Whitworth, Clink Finance Director

Serves 4 as a light lunch

Ingredients

400g Sunday lunch vegetable
leftovers (roast potatoes,
parsnips, carrots, cabbage,
peas... whatever!)
4 eggs, lightly beaten
1 tbsp vegetable oil

Method

• Chop the vegetables well and place in a large mixing bowl. Stir
in the eggs and enough water just to bind (just a splash).
• Heat the oil in a large heavy-based frying pan, tip in the
vegetable mixture and spread it out evenly.
• When the mixture has cooked enough to set (about 8 minutes),
wearing oven gloves, put a plate over the top and turn the frittata
out on to the plate. Slide it back into the pan to cook the other
side. Alternatively, place it under a preheated grill and cook until
the top is golden. Serve hot or cold with a green salad.

Roast vegetable pasta

Gemma Holford, Clink Marketing & PR

Ingredients

4 carrots, chopped
1 onion, chopped
1 red onion, chopped
1 courgette, chopped
250g tomatoes, halved
olive oil
50g rocket
250g fusilli
3 tbsp balsamic vinegar
1 tbsp light soy sauce
½ tsp sugar, or sweetener

Serves 2

Method

• Preheat the oven to 180°C (Gas 4).
• Lay all the vegetables, except the rocket, on a baking tray, add
a drizzle of oil, season to taste and roast for 25 minutes.
• Meanwhile, cook the fusilli according to the packet
instructions, then drain. Mix the balsamic vinegar, light soy
sauce and sugar or sweetener in a small bowl.
• Once the vegetables are cooked, put them in a mixing bowl.
Add the pasta, rocket and dressing and stir thoroughly,
then serve.

Roast vegetable salad

Jane Sanderson, Clink Director of Operations & Training

Serves 8–10 as a side dish

Ingredients

1 aubergine
4 colourful peppers (red, yellow, orange and green)
2 yellow courgettes
2 green courgettes
1 butternut squash, peeled, deseeded and chopped
12 radishes
2 red onions, cut into wedges

juice of 1 lemon
olive oil
100g marinated sun-dried tomatoes, chopped
100g marinated artichoke hearts, chopped
small can of pitted black olives
small bag of wild rocket
6 large basil leaves

Method

• Slice the aubergine, sprinkle with salt and leave in a colander for 20 minutes. Brush off the salt.
• Meanwhile, prepare all the other vegetables, cutting them into strips or halves, depending on size. Place a griddle pan over a high heat. When it is hot, dry-griddle the prepared vegetables until striped with black. Preheat the oven to 180°C (Gas 4).
• Place the vegetables in a roasting tin with the lemon juice and enough olive oil to coat them and toss thoroughly. Roast for 15–18 minutes. Halfway through, mix the vegetables very well. Remove from the oven and allow to rest for 5 minutes.
• Place in a serving bowl with the sun-dried tomatoes, artichokes, black olives and rocket. Add the basil, grind over black pepper and drizzle with the lemony olive oil from the roasting tin.

Tempura

Tim Wates, Clink Founder Trustee

Tim Wates is a director of Asian restaurant group Tampopo and they came up with this simplified tempura for him. Wonderful with our great British vegetables, and you can let your imagination run wild on dipping sauces.

Ingredients

100g cornflour
150g plain flour
10g baking powder
iced sparkling water
any vegetables you have: sweet potato, red onion, carrot, samphire and herbs are particularly good
flavourless vegetable oil

Method

• Mix both the flours together in a large bowl with the baking powder, making sure everything is evenly amalgamated.
• Gradually pour in iced sparkling water, stirring constantly, until you have a batter of a consistency that will coat your (clean) finger, should you dip it in. It doesn't matter at all if it's a bit lumpy, but do not over-mix!
• Chop your tempura ingredients into bite-sized pieces; chopping on the bias always looks good. Heat a large pan one-third full of flavourless vegetable oil until it is hot. If you have a cooking thermometer, it should read 180°C. Otherwise, throw in a drop of batter. If it sizzles immediately, the oil is ready.
• Dip the ingredients briefly in the batter and deep-fry, turning once, for a matter of minutes, just until very lightly golden and crisp. Meanwhile, mix all the ingredients for your dipping sauce.
• Drain on kitchen paper to blot off excess oil and serve immediately with the dipping sauce.

DIPPING SAUCE (SUGGESTED BY THE CLINK TEAM)

3 tbsp soy sauce
3 tbsp mirin
1 tbsp caster sugar
finely sliced red chilli
1 tbsp toasted sesame seeds

Sweet potato & chickpea salad

If you leave out the salad leaves (as we did for the photo), this makes an excellent side dish for spiced and seared meats or fish steaks.

Christa Janse van Rensburg, Head Chef Trainer, Clink Events

Serves 6

Ingredients

600g sweet potato, peeled and chopped

6 tbsp extra virgin olive oil, plus more for the garlic

1 garlic bulb

2 green chillies, deseeded and finely chopped

large handful of chopped coriander

400g can of chickpeas, drained and rinsed

1 preserved lemon, finely chopped

2 handfuls of crunchy salad leaves

sea salt and freshly ground black pepper

Method

• Preheat the oven to 220°C (Gas 7).

• Put the sweet potato in a roasting tin, toss with 2 tbsp of the oil to coat, then roast for about 20 minutes, or until it's cooked with a nice colour. Reduce the oven temperature to 160°C (Gas 3).

• Wrap the garlic bulb in foil, add 1 tbsp more oil and roast for about 45 minutes, or until the garlic is soft and sweet and you can squeeze it out of the bulb. Once it is cool enough to handle, squeeze out the garlic cloves.

• In a large salad bowl, mix the sweet potato, garlic and all the remaining ingredients together, not forgetting the remaining 3 tbsp olive oil, and season well with salt and pepper.

Aloo channa

Daniel Ayton, Clink Chef Ambassador

Serves 4 as a side dish

Ingredients

1 tbsp flavourless vegetable oil,
  plus more for the potatoes
2 tsp cumin seeds
1 tsp caraway seeds
½ tsp cloves
4 onions, finely chopped
100g potatoes, finely chopped
1 tbsp finely grated ginger
1 tbsp finely grated garlic
1 tbsp ground coriander

1 tsp chilli powder
1½ tsp garam masala
2 tbsp chana masala
2 chopped tomatoes
500g cooked chickpeas,
  drained and rinsed
1–2 tsp gram (chickpea) flour
juice of 1 lemon
handful of coriander leaves,
  chopped

Method

• Heat the oil in a sauté pan and, when hot, add the seeds and cloves until they sizzle and dance in the pan. Add the onions, cooking until they are soft and brown (be patient, this may take some time).

• At the same time, in a separate frying pan, fry the potatoes in more oil until they are tender. Set aside.

• Add the ginger and garlic pastes to the onion pan and cook just until they are fragrant, then add the ground spices and the tomatoes. Cook, stirring, until you can see the oil separating from the mixture in the pan.

• Stir in the cooked chickpeas. In a small cup, mix the gram flour with enough water to make a thin paste, then add this to the pan, stirring until the mixture has thickened.

• Add the potato, then finish with the lemon juice and coriander.

Vegetable korma

Alison Hulm, Clink Administration Manager

Serves 4

Ingredients

1 onion, finely chopped
4 tbsp vegetable oil
1 tbsp ground cumin
1 tsp ground turmeric
2 garlic cloves, finely chopped or grated
2.5cm piece of fresh root ginger, finely chopped or grated
1 green chilli, finely chopped, plus more to serve (optional)
300ml natural yogurt
45g ground almonds
sea salt
225g parsnips, sliced or chopped
340g carrots, sliced or chopped
225g cauliflower, divided into florets
flaked almonds, toasted, to serve

Method

• Fry the onion in the oil until soft. Add the ground spices and stir, then add the garlic, ginger and chilli. Gently fry for 1 minute.
• Slowly add the yogurt and the ground almonds. Cook for another minute, constantly stirring. Add a little water and season with salt.
• Next, add the vegetables, cover and simmer gently for 20–25 minutes until the vegetables are almost cooked. Then take the lid off and continue to cook for 5 minutes. Season to taste and serve, scattered with chilli, if you want, and almonds.

Onion bhaji

Serves 4 as a starter

Ingredients

2 eggs
3 onions, sliced
120g plain flour
1 tsp ground coriander
1 tsp cumin seeds
1 tbsp chopped coriander
vegetable oil, to deep-fry

Method

• Beat the eggs in a bowl. Add the sliced onions and mix well. Add the flour, spices and herbs and stir well to combine.

• Heat a large pan one-third full of flavourless vegetable oil until it is hot. If you have a cooking thermometer, it should read 180°C. Otherwise, throw in a drop of batter. If it sizzles immediately, the oil is ready.

• Add a large spoonful of the bhaji mixture and fry for 30–45 seconds, until golden brown. Turn the bhaji over with a slotted spoon and fry for a further 30 seconds, until crisp and golden brown all over. Remove and drain on kitchen paper.

• Repeat to cook the remaining bhaji mixture and serve immediately, with minted yogurt for dipping.

Aloo bhaji

Daniel Ayton, Clink Chef Ambassador

Serves 6 as a side dish

Ingredients

750g potato, peeled and cut
into 1cm dice

½ tsp ground turmeric

1 tsp flavourless vegetable
oil

½ tsp mustard seeds

½ tsp cumin seeds

2 bay leaves

2 curry leaves

100g onion, finely sliced

thumb-sized piece of fresh
root ginger, very finely
chopped, or grated

2 garlic cloves, finely sliced

1 green chilli, finely sliced

½ tsp chilli powder

1 tsp ground coriander

½ tsp ground cumin

½ tsp curry powder

125g tomatoes, chopped

sea salt

Method

• Boil the potato in a saucepan of water with the turmeric until slightly underdone. Set aside.

• Heat the oil in a sauté pan over a medium-high heat and, when hot, add the mustard seeds, cumin seeds, bay leaves and curry leaves. When they sizzle, add the sliced onion and fry until lightly brown, then add the ginger, garlic and green chilli and cook until you can see in the pan that the oil has separated from the mixture.

• Add the ground spices and the tomatoes, cooking them and pressing with a wooden spoon until they have mashed into the mixture. Now add the potatoes and cook until they are tender.

• Taste and adjust the salt, then serve.

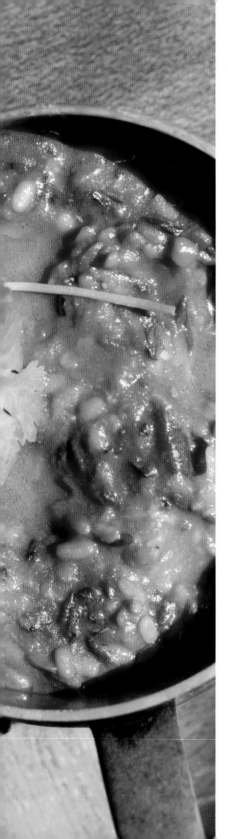

Dal makhani

Daniel Ayton, Clink Chef Ambassador

Serves 6–8

Ingredients

100g dried black lentils

50g dried kidney beans

2 large mild red chillies,
  deseeded

1 tsp ground turmeric

20g fresh root ginger

2 garlic cloves

1 tsp cumin seeds

1 tsp coriander seeds

2 tsp mild curry powder

80g ghee or unsalted butter

3 onions, finely chopped

1 cinnamon stick

8 green cardamom pods

sea salt and freshly ground
  black pepper

2 tsp caster sugar

2 tbsp malt vinegar

600g tomatoes, finely chopped

600ml vegetable stock

finely grated zest and juice of
  1 unwaxed lemon

4 tbsp coriander leaves,
  chopped

Method

• The night before, soak the lentils and kidney beans in 4 times their volume of cold water. When ready to cook, drain them.

• Use a blender to mince the chillies, turmeric, ginger, garlic, cumin and coriander seeds and curry powder to a paste.

• Heat a large saucepan with 50g of the ghee and sauté the onions, cinnamon and cardamom until golden brown. Now add the curry paste and sauté for 2 minutes. Add the pulses, stir and season. Sauté for 1 minute, then add the sugar and vinegar and cook for 1 minute, stirring. Add the tomatoes and stock, bring to a simmer, cover and cook for 30 minutes, stirring occasionally.

• Uncover and cook for 10 minutes. I like dal quite dry, but if you prefer it soupy, stop cooking once the lentils are cooked. Melt the remaining ghee and stir it in with the zest, juice and coriander.

Butter beans in sesame & ginger gravy

Duncan Bell, Clink Friend

Serves 4

Ingredients

2 tsp cumin seeds

1½ tbsp vegetable oil

1 large onion, chopped

250g mushrooms, sliced

2 carrots, sliced

1 green pepper, chopped

300ml apple juice

1½ tbsp soy sauce

2 x 400g cans of butter beans,
    drained and rinsed

3cm fresh root ginger,
    finely grated

2½ tbsp tahini

Method

• Toast the cumin seeds over a medium heat in a dry frying pan until they've turned a shade darker. Keep swirling them in the pan to prevent them burning. When they're ready, tip them into a mortar and pestle or spice grinder and grind them to a powder.

• Meanwhile, heat the oil in a large saucepan, add the onion and cook over a low heat until softened, stirring regularly.

• Now increase the heat to medium, add the mushrooms, carrots and pepper and cook until the mushrooms start to soften. Then add the ground cumin and cook for another 1–2 minutes until the mushrooms have softened, stirring regularly.

• Add the apple juice and soy sauce, cover and simmer gently for 15–20 minutes until the carrots and pepper are nearly tender. Finally, stir in the drained beans, ginger and tahini and simmer for another 5 minutes.

• Serve with rice or couscous.

Potato gnocchi with scamorza & basil

Daniel Ayton, Clink Chef Ambassador

Serves 4

Ingredients

FOR THE GNOCCHI

500g waxy potatoes, ideally Ratte

coarse sea salt

30g '00' pasta flour, plus more to coat

1 egg, lightly beaten

FOR THE SAUCE

4 tsp olive oil, plus more to serve

4 tsp garlic-flavoured olive oil

6 plum tomato petals (quartered and
   deseeded tomatoes)

3 basil leaves, plus more to serve

½ tsp sea salt

20g Parmesan cheese, finely grated

20g scamorza cheese, finely chopped

8 cherry tomato petals

4 tsp vegetable stock

Method

• Preheat the oven to 160°C (Gas 3).

• Place the potatoes on a layer of coarse sea salt on a baking tray and roast for 40 minutes, or until soft in the middle. Once cooked, remove the potato skins and either pass through a mouli (vegetable mill), or mash thoroughly.

• On a cool work surface, combine the potato with the flour and egg. Knead with your hands until the mixture forms a firm dough. Allow to stand for a couple of minutes.

• Roll the dough into thin sausages and cut at 2.5cm intervals. To stop the gnocchi from sticking together, coat them in flour and set aside on a sheet of baking parchment.

• Now for the sauce. In a small saucepan, heat the olive oil and garlic oil. Add the plum tomato petals, the basil and salt and sauté for 1 minute.

• Meanwhile, place the gnocchi into rapidly boiling salted water and cook for 3 minutes. The gnocchi will float once cooked. Drain very well.

• Add the gnocchi to the tomatoes with the Parmesan. Once melted and fully incorporated, season and finish with the scamorza, cherry tomato petals and stock.

• Serve once the scamorza has melted, drizzled with a little olive oil and scattered with basil.

Clear beetroot soup (Barszcz czysty czerwony)

Rosie Tryka, Clink Friend

This easy clear soup gets the desired hint of sourness from lemon juice and is great eaten hot or cold with rye bread. This meatless soup is often served with mushroom or meat dumplings for a Polish Christmas Eve dinner.

Serves 4

Ingredients

4 beetroots
1 litre vegetable stock
1 garlic clove, finely chopped
1 teaspoon sugar (any kind is fine)
2 tablespoons lemon juice
sea salt and freshly ground black pepper
handful of dill, chopped (optional)
sour cream, to serve (optional)

Method

• Preheat the oven to 200°C (Gas 6).
• Wrap the beetroots in foil and roast until tender, 30–45 minutes. When cool enough to handle, peel and slice into strips or julienne.
• In a saucepan, bring the vegetable stock to the boil, add the beetroots, garlic, sugar and lemon juice with salt and pepper to taste. Simmer for 10 minutes.
• Serve hot, scattered with dill. This is good hot with boiled potatoes on the side, or cool quickly in an ice-water bath and refrigerate to serve cold, with dill and sour cream.

Puddings

Rhubarb crumble cake

Alison Hulm, Clink Administration Manager

Swap out up to one-third of the flour for ground almonds,
if you like, for a slightly moister sponge.

Serves 9

Ingredients

FOR THE CAKE

175g unsalted butter, softened,
    plus more for the tin
300g rhubarb
juice of ½ lemon
165g self-raising flour
175g caster sugar
3 large eggs
2 tsp vanilla extract

FOR THE CRUMBLE

20g unsalted butter, cut
    into cubes
50g self-raising flour
20g caster sugar
2 tsp ground ginger

Method

• Preheat the oven to 180°C (Gas 4). Butter a 23cm square cake tin and line the base with baking parchment.

• Trim and chop the rhubarb into 3cm pieces, mix with the lemon juice and set aside.

• In a separate bowl, whisk together the flour, butter, sugar, eggs and vanilla, using an electric whisk. Fold in half the rhubarb and spoon the mixture into the prepared tin, spreading it out with a spatula. Scatter over the rest of the rhubarb.

• Now, for the topping, rub the butter into the flour in a large bowl until the mixture resembles crumbs, then stir in the sugar and ginger. Sprinkle the crumble over the cake mixture and bake for 50 minutes.

• Leave to cool for 10 minutes, then remove from the tin, slice into squares and serve warm or cold.

Aubergine chocolate cake

Serves 8

Ingredients

a little flavourless oil

2 small whole aubergines,
   about 400g total weight

300g good-quality dark
   chocolate, broken up

50g good-quality cocoa
   powder, plus more to serve

60g ground almonds

3 eggs

200g clear honey

2 tsp baking powder

¼ tsp salt

1 tbsp brandy

Method

• Preheat the oven to 180°C (Gas 4). Line a 23cm loose-bottomed tin with baking parchment and lightly brush with oil.

• Pierce the aubergines with a skewer, then place in a bowl covered in cling film. Microwave on high for 8 minutes until limp, then skin and purée the flesh in a blender.

• Add the chocolate. Set aside, covered once again in cling film, until the chocolate has melted. (You may need to microwave it again for 1 minute, covered in cling film, on the lowest setting.)

• In a large bowl, whisk all the other ingredients for a minute until slightly frothy. Fold in the aubergine mix, pour into the tin and cook at the bottom of the oven for 30 minutes.

• Let cool in the tin for 15 minutes, then turn out on to a wire rack and peel off the parchment. Quickly turn it the right way up again and sit it on a plate. Sift over a little cocoa powder to serve.

Cezerye (Turkish delight with carrot)

Daniel Ayton, Clink Chef Ambassador

Makes enough for 6–8 as an after-dinner nibble

Ingredients

400g carrots, finely grated

200g brown or white granulated sugar

2 tsp ground cinnamon

1 tsp vanilla extract

100g walnuts, roughly chopped (optional)

coconut flakes, to coat

Method

• Line a small baking tray with baking parchment.

• Put the carrots and sugar into a saucepan. Add about 240ml of water and cook over a medium heat until the carrots start to melt and the mixture is thickened. (When you take a piece and roll it into a ball between your thumb and finger, it should stick to one finger only.) Stir in the cinnamon and vanilla.

• Add the walnuts, if you want.

• Using a silicone spatula, spread the mixture into the prepared tray to 1cm thick. Cover and chill for 1 hour to thicken further.

• Using a wet knife (so the cezerye doesn't stick to it), cut into 1 x 2.5cm rectangles. Spread the coconut on a plate and roll the cut-out sweets in it to coat. Store in the fridge.

Cherry clafoutis

Debbie Whitworth, Clink Finance Director

Serves 6

Ingredients

40g unsalted butter, melted and cooled, plus more for the tin
50g plain flour
70g caster sugar
3 eggs, lightly beaten
200ml double cream
300g cherries, pitted and halved

Method

• Preheat the oven to 160°C (Gas 3). Butter a 20cm cake tin, or ovenproof cast-iron pan.
• Sift the flour into a large bowl, add the sugar and mix together with the eggs and cream. Add the melted butter and stir well until combined.
• Scatter the cherries over the base of the cake tin, pour the batter over the cherries and bake for 30 minutes, or until golden brown. Serve with lots of crème fraîche.

Courgette & lemon thyme cake

Natasha Morgan, Clink Friend

Makes 1 loaf cake

Ingredients

125ml vegetable oil, plus more
  for the tin
3 large courgettes, finely
  grated
3 eggs, lightly beaten
150g caster sugar
250g plain flour
1 tsp bicarbonate of soda
1 tsp baking powder
1 tsp lemon thyme leaves

Method

• Preheat the oven to 180°C (Gas 4). Oil a 450g loaf tin and line it with baking parchment. Put the courgettes in a clean tea towel and squeeze them over a sink until all the moisture is removed.
• Put the oil, eggs and sugar in a large bowl and beat until creamy. Sift in the flour, bicarbonate of soda and baking powder and continue to beat until combined. Stir in the courgettes and lemon thyme.
• Pour into the prepared tin and bake for 50–60 minutes. Remove from the oven and leave in the tin for 5 minutes. Turn on to a wire rack and allow to cool.

Sweet potato & white chocolate cake

Annie Fort, General Manager Trainer, The Clink High Down

Makes 2 loaf cakes

Ingredients

90ml vegetable oil

150g white chocolate, in
  small chunks

250g self-raising flour

200g caster sugar

250g sweet potato, peeled
  and cut into chunks

4 eggs

1 tsp vanilla extract

Method

• Preheat the oven to 180°C (Gas 4). Line 2 x 450g loaf tins with baking parchment.

• Place the oil and half the chocolate in a heatproof bowl over simmering water. Do not let the bowl touch the water. Stir occasionally until the mixture has melted and is smooth.

• Sift the flour into a large bowl, then stir in the sugar.

• Purée the raw sweet potatoes in a blender, then add the eggs one at a time. Add the vanilla, then the melted oil mixture.

• Pour the oil mixture over the flour mixture and stir well, then stir in the remaining chocolate. Scrape into the prepared tins.

• Cook for 50 minutes to 1 hour; a cocktail stick inserted into the centres should come out dry. Cool, then turn out of the tins.

Basil pannacotta with strawberries

Serves 6

Ingredients

1 sachet (7g) powdered gelatine
250ml skimmed milk
1 tbsp grated orange zest
4 tbsp clear honey, or to taste
leaves from a large bunch of basil
480g Greek yogurt
225g strawberries, quartered
½ tsp lemon juice
2 tbsp caster sugar

Method

• In a small bowl, sprinkle the gelatine over 3 tbsp of the milk and allow to soften.
• Heat the remaining milk in a saucepan until it is about to simmer, but has not yet reached boiling point. Add the orange zest and half the honey, stir and taste. Add the remaining honey if you prefer it sweeter.
• Blanch the basil leaves in boiling water for 25 seconds, then refresh in ice-cold water. Squeeze the basil to remove the water and add it to the honey-sweetened milk.
• Pour the basil milk into a blender and pulse until smooth. Strain the mixture through a sieve and place it in a clean saucepan. Heat again to just before boiling, then add the gelatine milk, remove from the heat and whisk until the gelatine has completely melted.
• Stir in the yogurt and mix well. Check for sweetness, adding more honey if you wish.
• Pour into 6 glasses or ramekins and place in the fridge for a minimum of 4 hours.
• For the topping, mix the strawberries, lemon juice and caster sugar and place in a covered bowl in the fridge for not more than 1 hour.
• If you are using ramekins, run a sharp knife around the edges and turn out on to plates to serve. Otherwise, just serve the pannacottas in the glasses, spooning the macerated strawberries on top.

Beetroot & rose cupcakes

Daniel Ayton, Clink Chef Ambassador

Makes 12

Ingredients

FOR THE CUPCAKES

175g caster sugar

175g unsalted butter, softened

3 eggs, separated

175g self-raising flour

175g puréed cooked beetroot, drained (keep a few drops of juice back for colouring)

1 tbsp vanilla extract

FOR THE ICING

300g icing sugar

150g unsalted butter, softened

rose water, to taste

beetroot juice, to colour

unsprayed rose petals, or dried rose petals, to serve

Method

• Preheat the oven to 180°C (Gas 4).

• Blend together the sugar and butter until light and creamy. Add the egg yolks, flour, puréed beetroot and vanilla and beat until smooth.

• In a clean bowl, whisk the egg whites until fairly stiff. Take a large spoonful of egg whites and beat into the cupcake mixture to loosen it a little. Then, using a large metal spoon, fold the remaining egg whites gently through the mix.

• Spoon the mixture into 12 cupcake cases and bake in the oven for 10–15 minutes, or until the cakes are firm to the touch. Remove and cool on a wire rack.

• To make the icing, beat the icing sugar and butter, either in a food mixer or with a wooden spoon. Add a few drops of rose water to taste and a few drops of beetroot juice to colour.

• Spread generously or pipe over the cooled cupcakes and top with rose petals.

Pear sorbet

This recipe can also be used to make apple sorbet, too,
just replace the pears with 5 sweet dessert apples.

Serves 4

Ingredients

5 small sweet English pears,
   peeled, cored and sliced
180ml sweet white wine,
   or apple juice
75g caster sugar
5 tsp lemon juice

Method

• In a large saucepan, combine all the ingredients and bring
to the boil over a high heat. Reduce the heat and simmer,
uncovered, for 8–10 minutes, or until the pears are tender.
Cool slightly.
• Pour into a food processor, cover and process until smooth.
Transfer to a freezerproof dish, cover and freeze for 4 hours,
or until firm.
• Just before serving, process again in a food processor for
1–2 minutes, or until smooth. Spoon into dessert dishes.

Spiced berry compote

Debbie Whitworth, Clink Finance Director

Serves 4–6, with the sorbet above, or porridge or yogurt

Ingredients

500g mixed berries
   (frozen is fine)
caster sugar, to taste
ground cinnamon, to taste

Method

• Put the berries in a saucepan, add 2–3 tbsp of water and bring
to the boil. Cook for 3 minutes, then taste and sweeten with
sugar, if you want. Add the cinnamon to taste. Chill, then serve.

Preserves

Giardiniera (garden pickles)

Finlay Scott, Clink Chairman and Founder trustee

Makes 2 x 340g jars

Ingredients

3 spring onions

1½ celery stalks

1 carrot

100g pickling cucumbers

150g peppers, a mixture of
    whatever you fancy

⅛ cauliflower

400ml white wine vinegar

2 tbsp granulated sugar

1½ tbsp coarse sea salt

9 black peppercorns

2 bay leaves

Method

• To begin, rinse and prepare all the vegetables. Slice each spring onion into 3 pieces equal in length. Slice the celery into pieces no more than 1cm thick. Peel the carrot and slice into thin rounds about 4mm thick, using a mandolin if possible. Do the same for the unpeeled cucumbers. Slice open the peppers, remove the stem, seeds and pith, and slice into medium-thin strips. Remove the thick stalk from the cauliflower and cut away small florets

• Fill a large, deep pan with water. Place your chosen jars and their lids inside and bring to a low boil for 12 minutes.

• Bring the vinegar and 400ml water to the boil in another large saucepan. Add the sugar, salt, peppercorns and bay leaves. When some of the water has evaporated, add the carrot and cauliflower and boil for 2 minutes. Lift the vegetables from the liquid using a slotted spoon and transfer to a bowl.

• Next, add the spring onions, celery, and peppers and cook for another 2–3 minutes. Remove. Lastly, add the cucumbers and boil for 1 minute. Remove. Retain the cooking liquid.

• Remove the jars from their pan and set on a tea towel. When the vegetables are cool, transfer them to the jars without packing them in too much (a small soup ladle works well). Strain the warm cooking liquid and pour it over the vegetables, leaving a gap of about 2.5cm from the top of each jar. Seal the jars.

• Return the jars to the large deep pan and add water to 2.5cm above the tops of the jars. Bring to the boil for 30 minutes.

• Remove the jars from the water with tongs and set aside to cool. When the jars are completely cooled, test the seal and firmly tighten the lid. Store for at least 1 month before opening. The pickle can be stored for up to 3 months in a cool, dry place away from the light. Consume within 3 days of opening.

Plum jam

Makes about 4kg, scale it down if you wish

Ingredients

2.7kg plums, washed, stalks removed

2.7kg granulated sugar

lemon juice, to taste

Method

• Put a clean saucer in the freezer. Hot-wash and then sterilise the jam jars, by placing in an oven preheated to 140°C (Gas 1) for 30 minutes.

• Meanwhile, place the whole plums in a saucepan and pour in 900ml of water. Bring to the boil, then reduce the heat and simmer for 30 minutes. The fruit should become soft and the contents of the pan much reduced. Remove the pan from the heat, add the sugar and stir well until dissolved.

• Return the pan to the heat, bring to the boil and taste, adding lemon juice to taste (it should be a little tart). Continue to boil for 10–15 minutes, stirring.

• Test for a set: spoon a little of the jam on to the cold saucer and push your finger against it. If the jam goes crinkly-wrinkly, it is solid enough and the set is reached. (If not, continue cooking for a few minutes, then test again.) Take the pan off the heat.

• Using a slotted spoon, remove the stones and any scum from the surface of the jam. Leave to stand for 15 minutes.

• Ladle the jam into the sterilised, warm jars and seal while it is still hot.

Medlar or quince jelly

Makes 4–5 x 340g jars

Ingredients

1.8kg medlars or quinces, chopped
juice of 2 lemons
800g–1kg granulated sugar

Method

• In a large saucepan, boil the medlars or quinces in 2 litres of water over a high heat, then reduce the heat and cover. Simmer slowly for about 45 minutes, then turn off the heat and mash the fruit.

• Put the mashed fruit into a muslin bag and hang it over a bowl. Leave overnight. Though it is tempting to do so, do not squeeze the bag, or the jelly will become cloudy. Next morning, add the lemon juice to the collected juice in the bowl.

• For every 250ml juice you collect, add 200g sugar. Return to the cleaned-out pan and cook over a low heat, gradually increasing the temperature until the mixture is boiling. Boil for 25 minutes, or until setting point is reached (see page 100).

• Pour into sterilised warm jars (see page 100) and seal while it is still hot.

Redcurrant & rosemary jelly

Makes 10 x 340g jars

Ingredients

3kg redcurrants
3kg granulated sugar
small bunch of rosemary

Method

• Wash the fruit and place in a saucepan, stalks and all. Bring to the boil, pressing down on the currants with a spoon to release their juice.
• After 10 minutes, add the sugar and rosemary and stir until dissolved. Bring to the boil and boil rapidly for 8 minutes, or until setting point is reached (see page 100).
• Pour into sterilised warm jars (see page 100) and seal while it is still hot.

Balsamic onion marmalade

Makes 1–2 x 340g jars

Ingredients

6 red onions, sliced
olive oil
4 garlic cloves, finely chopped
250ml balsamic vinegar
bunch of thyme, tied with string
200g caster sugar

Method

• Sweat the onions in a little olive oil until beginning to caramelise. This will take longer than you think, but be patient.

• Add the garlic and cook for 2 minutes, but don't let it turn brown, or it will taste bitter.

• Add the balsamic vinegar and thyme, bring to the boil, then add the sugar. Immediately reduce the heat and simmer until the marmalade thickens.

• Remove the thyme and pour into sterilised warm jars (see page 100) and seal while it is still hot.

Al's tomato passata

It is preferable to make this outside on a barbecue or an open fire pit as my mother does, this way you avoid pebble-dashing your kitchen with tomatoes and you can use a bigger pot. You will need glass jars with lids, or Kilner jars.

Makes as much as you have tomatoes (good for a glut)

Ingredients
ripe or slightly over-ripe tomatoes, as many
  as you have
garlic
basil
olive oil

Method
• Take the biggest pot you have and half-fill it with whole tomatoes. Add 1 peeled garlic clove and 4 basil leaves per 2kg of tomatoes. Cover with water and bring to the boil, then reduce the heat and simmer slowly for 2 hours, stirring frequently to avoid burning. Add more water if it gets too thick.
• After 2 hours, it should be bubbling like molten lava. Pass through a mouli-legumes (a vegetable mill). Pour into warm sterilised jars (see page 100), leaving a 2cm gap from the rim. Push a peeled garlic clove and a basil leaf into each jar and pour in enough olive oil to cover by 5mm. Seal.
• Place into the washed pot and cover the jars with cold water. Bring to the boil slowly, then reduce the heat and simmer for 45 minutes. Leave to cool in the water overnight, then store in a cool, dry, dark place. This happily lasts a year.

Tomato marmalade

Makes 3 x 340g jars

Ingredients

1 large onion, chopped
olive oil
5kg ripe or over-ripe tomatoes, chopped
4 garlic cloves, chopped
pinch of mixed spice
250ml balsamic vinegar
250g granulated sugar
bunch of basil
sea salt and freshly ground black pepper

Method

• In a large saucepan, sweat the onion in a little olive oil. Add the tomatoes and garlic and cook until they soften. Add the mixed spice and vinegar and bring to the boil.

• Add the sugar, reduce the heat and simmer until it dissolves. Tear the basil leaves into the pan and then simmer for a final 10 minutes, or until the marmalade thickens. Season to taste.

• Pour into warm sterilised jars (see page 100) and seal while it is still hot. In a cool, dry, dark place, this will keep for at least 6 months.

Limoncello

Christopher Moore, Clink Chief Executive

Makes about 1.5 litres

Ingredients
finely grated zest of
   12 unwaxed lemons
1 litre vodka
650g caster sugar

Method
• Put the lemon zest into a large glass bottle (or jug). Pour in the vodka. Sit the cap on the top of the bottle (or jug), but don't screw it on. Leave it for 1 week at room temperature.
• Place the sugar in a saucepan and pour in 1 litre of water. Set over a medium heat and bring to the boil, but don't stir. Boil for 15 minutes, then turn off the heat and leave the syrup to cool.
• Strain the infused vodka into the syrup. Bottle in glass bottles and seal them with a screwtop or cork. Leave for at least 2 weeks at room temperature.
• To serve, place the bottled liqueur in the freezer. Once chilled, serve it in chilled or frozen small or shot glasses.

Sloe gin

Debbie Whitworth, Clink Finance Director

Makes 750ml

Ingredients
500g sloes
225g caster sugar
1 bottle of gin

Method
• Prick the skins of the sloes with a clean needle, then put them in a sterilised jar (see page 100). Add the sugar, then pour in the gin. It should cover the fruit, but leave a gap of 3cm at the top.
• Seal the jar, shake well and leave in a cool, dark place for about 2 months, shaking from time to time. When finished, strain the gin from the fruit and pour into glass bottles.

Index

First published in Great Britain in 2018 by The Clink Trading

A CIP catalogue record for this title is available from the British Library
ISBN 978-0-9933569-3-3

Publisher: Alison Cathie
Editor: Lucy Bannell
Photography and design: Ros Holder
Foreword (pages 4–5) and jacket flap
portrait photography: David Cummings;
foreword (pages 4–5) food photography: Paul Griffiths
Home economist: Nicola Roberts
Home economist's assistant: Esther Clark
Proofreader: Kathy Steer
Indexer: Vicki Robinson
PR and marketing: Gemma Holford
Project manager: Christopher Moore

Printed and bound in China
by 1010 International Printing Limited

The Clink Trading
HMP High Down
High Down Lane
Sutton
Surrey
SM2 5PJ

www.theclinkcharity.org

We would like to thank Al Crisci and all our
recipe contributors, and also Christopher
Moore. Particular thanks to Alison Cathie,
Ros Holder and Lucy Bannell, for the
beautiful book they've put together. Very
many thanks, too, to Gemma Holford.

The biodegradable, eco-friendly bamboo
serveware shown in this book is by Bambu
from www.asliceofgreen.co.uk.